THE BLESSING of Serving Another Man's Ministry

CW01582622

Dear Jeanne, Thank you for your ministry! God Bless, Greg Heb 6:10

SEVEN SERVING SECRETS THAT WILL SENTENCE YOU TO SUCCESS!

GREG MAURO

Second Edition

PUBLISHED BY
Greg Mauro
Copyright© 2012
San Diego, California
Printed in the United States of America.

Quoted verses of scripture throughout this book may have been taken from any of the publications below, and we therefore wish to credit them:

The Holy Bible, Authorized King James Version
Used with permission from THE GIDEONS International
1958 Edition, by The National Bible Press, Printed in the USA

The Holy Bible, New King James Version ("NKJV")
Copyright © 1982 and 1994, by Thomas Nelson, Inc., Printed in the USA

The Holy Bible, New International Version ("NIV")
Copyright © 1973, 1978, and 1984, by International Bible Society

The Holy Bible, New American Standard Bible ("NASB")
Copyright © 1960, 1962, 1963, 1968, 1971, 1973, 1975, 1977, 1995
THE LOCKMAN FOUNDATION, A Corporation Not For Profit

The Holy Bible, The Amplified Bible ("AMP")
Copyright © 1954, 1958, 1962, 1964, 1965, 1987
by The Lockman Foundation

The Holy Bible, The Living Bible ("TLB"), Paraphrased
Copyright © 1971, by Tyndale House Publishers, Wheaton, IL 60187

The Holy Bible, The Oxford Annotated Bible, Revised Standard Version ("RSV")
Copyright © 1962, by Oxford University Press, Inc., Division of Christian Education of the National Council of Churches of Christ in the United States of America

All scripture quotations are taken from the Authorized King James Version of the Bible, unless otherwise noted.

All quotations of scripture have been modified with emphasis by the adding of italics. There are places within the quoted scriptures that may have an open quote without a close quote (or vice versa) or an open parenthesis without a close parenthesis (or vice versa) or a word with a capital letter in the middle of a sentence. These are not typographical errors or oversights. They are exact quotes from the versions that we are using.

Table of Contents

Foreword

It has been one of the great joys of our lives for Theresa and I to watch the anointing of God increase upon Greg's life these past twenty five years.

Greg has become more than a blessing – he is a dear spiritual son and an extension of my ministry. His life has literally demonstrated the message in the pages of "The Blessing of Serving Another Man's Ministry." He has flourished as he has served and received the impartation from my life and ministry to his.

Those that come under the special anointing imparted in this book truly become an extension of what it really means to be a disciple of Christ.

God called Greg as an accounting student from Oral Roberts University with a passion to reach the world for Jesus, to come and join the Morris Cerullo World Evangelism team in San Diego in 1987.

As he showed himself faithful over time, I will never forget then sending him to live in England with his young family as my European Director for almost seven years. Together we saw Great Britain shaken as 16,000 plus a night jammed the historic Earl's Court Auditorium for annual week-long Mission to London meetings, 50,000 pack the Olympic Stadium over three nights in Moscow, Russia, just months after the Iron Curtain came down, pioneer Christian television across Europe and so much more...

Over the years, Greg has served as my crusade director, television co-host, writer, accountant, media buyer, marketing and public relations man, emcee of my conferences, and most of all my associate minister.

Ever pastor – leader – believer — that wants God to use their life in a greater way – will be deeply blessed and enriched by the encouraging words of this book.

I highly recommend every pastor and spiritual leader who truly wants an armor bearer, to seed this message into their lives. You will be rewarded with a ministry of faithfulness.

God's servant,

Morris Cerullo

Dedication

To be honest, as I wrestled with the promptings to write this short book for the past several years, many times I would say, "God, the last thing we need in the world today is another book for Christians!"

Then as we entered 2012, I realized that I was embarking on the 25th anniversary of serving an incredible man of God, and that this book could really serve two unique purposes. One, to honor my mentor by sharing just a tip of the ice berg of what has been imparted to me and how much this experience has meant to me personally. And in so doing perhaps to serve in a small way to pull back the veil and contribute to the overall legacy and impact of the life and ministry of Dr Morris Cerullo.

Secondly, I decided that I wouldn't write some preaching or theoretical book. God has allowed me to have a unique personal experience that I pray could serve as an encouragement for anyone of any age that simply has a desire to be used by God. Maybe God would use this book to spark someone that sat where I sat 25 years ago, with a passion to make a difference in their generation, and present to you the exciting blessing that can await you as you consider answering the calling to serve another's ministry...

To say this treatise would not have been possible without the providence of God allowing me the privilege and opportunity twenty-five years ago to serve the many faceted ministry of Morris Cerullo, would appear to be self-evident. What has meant the most to me is not just being welcomed to the incredible ministry of this great man, but the awesome privilege of being embraced by Morris and Theresa Cerullo as a son.

Their consistent example of integrity, compassion, counsel and concern for me and for my family has been one of the great privileges and unexpected blessings of my life.

While serving this man and this ministry has been the passion, joy and privilege of my life these years, and has not been without it's challenges and sacrifices, it is crystal clear to me that as much as I have given, I have received infinitely more. That would not have been possible if God had not connected me to a man whose heart was not to simply hire an employee, but to impart the anointing and wisdom from his life into the life of a mentor and a son.

For that I will be eternally grateful.

I would also be remiss if I didn't acknowledge the staff and executive team of Morris Cerullo World Evangelism. Much of what I have been able to accomplish has been because of their partnership as co-laborers in the ministry. I don't think there is a better, more dedicated ministry team anywhere.

Finally, to my wife Jeri, who is my best friend, co-laborer, biggest encourager, example and inspiration; God surely out did Himself when He brought her into my life! And my eight incredible children that have shared their father with the world and brought me endless pride and joy. I love each one of you and am so proud of each one of you.

SECRET
1

Settling the Question: *Is There A Ministry Of Serving Another Man's Ministry?*

The place: I will forever remember as though we were standing there now as you read these words...

The walking bridge connecting the student parking lot to the bustling campus of Oral Roberts University, where the grandiose buildings and space age architecture were a daily reminder to the thousands of us students of Dr Oral Roberts charge to "Make no small plans here".

The time: Twenty five years ago.

The experience: A life changing encounter that would set the course for my spiritual future in ways I would never have imagined when I woke up almost late for class that beautiful Spring morning in Tulsa...

With a mere six weeks remaining before graduation, and with a dream in my heart far bigger than myself, I was ready to go from this incredible place of preparation to be used by God to fulfill the Great Commission and reach our world for Christ.

Serving as a youth pastor in a local church, as a worship leader in another, carrying a 10 foot cross and sharing the gospel with whomever would listen across Tulsa, preaching on the streets, outside bars, leading evangelistic teams to Florida's beaches during Spring break to witness to the masses of college students that swarm there from across the country—now coupled with my ORU experience, I was ready to spread my wings and take the next exciting step in God's unfolding plan.

I drove my old car from the student apartments to campus, parked in the lot outside the Mabee Center and began my trek to class.

Done it hundreds of times. Grab my books, slam the car door closed and begin my brisk walk with a spring in my step to be sure I get to the first class of the day on time.

Connecting the parking lot and the campus is a simple white cement walking bridge spanning across a creek that divides the lot from the ORU campus, a well traveled daily route...

But I was soon to find out that this day would be unlike any other.

As I set foot on the bridge, I encountered a tangible presence and heard a voice that I knew only to well—that stopped me in my tracks...

Students scurrying to class by the scores walked past me as I stood still at the mid point of this small bridge.

Perhaps a minute passed, and now I was standing alone on the bridge.

Unexpectedly stopped by a wonderful presence and challenged by the unmistakable voice of the Holy Spirit.

The words as fresh today as they were 25 years ago,

"Greg, what would you think if I called you to serve another man's ministry that had the same vision that I have put in

your heart, and by doing so, you would reach more people for My kingdom than if you did so on your own?"

I stood motionless pondering this heavenly proposition.

A few straggling students passed by on the bridge I'm sure wondering if this skinny 6' 9" motionless statue of a fellow student had lost his marbles!

Knowing how I responded to this divine moment would surely set the course for God's future plans for my life.

And marveling what a gentleman our God is...

To present a "what would you think?" question, and not some "thus saith the Lord, you will do such and such..." command!

I stood there and pondered...

Give up the idea of launching "my own" ministry...

Serve someone else's ministry that had the same heart as I do.

Reach more people.

Be more effective for the Kingdom of God.

The more I mulled it over, it was a clear no brainer!

"Sure, Lord. If I can be more fruitful and reach more for You by helping someone else that is already doing what You have put in my heart to do, then count me in!"

Two weeks later, the ORU chapel service guest minister was introduced to the students, worldwide evangelist, apostle, prophet, Dr Morris Cerullo.

Another life changing encounter...

As this servant of God spoke from the words of John 6:28 *"What must we do that we might work the works of God",* the Mabee Center chapel shook as the anointing of the Holy Spirit was poured out mightily upon the students.

Soon all were out of their seats, dropped to their knees, and crying out for God to use their lives...

As was I.

As I slowly began to stand after this season of prayer and communion with God in this powerful chapel service, that same voice I encountered on the bridge spoke again,

"Greg, I am calling you to stand by Morris' side and help him in the ministry."

Immediately my plans to enroll in the ORU seminary that Fall flashed before my minds eye. I asked God, "What about my plans to attend seminary?"

Now a quarter of a century later, God's four word reply has proven over and over again to be the understatement of my life,

"This will be greater!"

On my knees in that ORU chapel service, I could not have imagined the blessings that God had in store these past 25 years serving as the vice-president of Ministries for Dr Morris Cerullo.

A beautiful, godly wife. Eight incredible, healthy children. By the grace of God and their hard work each offered full scholarships to attend some of the top universities in the world. Three adorable grand children. A praying mother that loves and prays for me and our family and the ministry of Dr Cerullo in her prayers daily. A younger brother, Glenn that has a heart of gold and another brother, Gary, that pastors one of the great churches in America...

The opportunity to stand by Dr Cerullo's side as communism fell (as he prophesied for 14 consecutive years prior from the platform of the Royal Albert Hall) and conduct the first historic public crusade in Moscow before 50,000 in the Olympic Stadium...

To stand by Dr Cerullo's 'side and give birth to week-long Mission to London outreaches from world famous Earl's Court to capacity crowds of 16,000 per night for six successive years, that shook Britain and garnered unprecedented national and worldwide attention for the message of the power of the gospel of Jesus Christ...

To personally preach by a spontaneous miracle to 200,000 protestors on the University Square in Bucharest, Romania following the fall of the dictator Nicolae Ceausescu while I was in there meeting with key leaders that had invited Dr Cerullo to conduct a national School of Ministry and Crusade later that year...

Now on my fourth passport, having been privileged to see millions saved, healed, set free, receive the impartation of the anointing and being used by God on every continent... Yes, there is unquestionably an incredible blessing waiting for those that will rise up to accept the calling to serve another man's ministry.

To do so we will have to rise above a culture and an era that celebrates the entrepreneur, the self-made man or woman that blazes his or her own trail. That same spirit has permeated the church, particularly the independent, Charismatic segments, where we are frequently bombarded with all the messages, encouragements, "words from the

Lord" and marketing tools to launch your own ministry – get ordained – start your website – launch your own worldwide ministry and go!

In sharp contrast, Jesus said, *"And if ye have not been faithful in that which is another man's, who shall give you that which is your own?"* (Luke 16:22)

If we agree that there is a calling to serve another man's ministry, then it is my prayer that many will rise up from their church pew as a spectator each Sunday and find an exciting, blessed place of service along side the ministry they are a part of.

I Corinthians 12:28 highlights the importance of the ministry of helps in the God-ordained structure of the church, listing it right after apostles, prophets, teachers, miracles, gifts of healings:

And God has appointed these in the church: first apostles, second prophets, third teachers, after that miracles, then gifts of healings, ***helps,*** *administrations, varieties of tongues.*

Kim Harrington of Masterbuilder Ministries said it so well in her article on "The Ministry of Helps":

"People approach the church with pretty much the same consumer mentality they bring to the shopping mall — you better deliver the goods, be nice and user-friendly, or I'll simply take my business elsewhere. The concept of servanthood and faithfulness, sacrifice and dependability seems to be a thing of the past, or at least something that doesn't apply to church anymore.

The desperate need in all sorts of Christian ministries is for those who will dedicate themselves to the ministry of helps, a rather inglorious sounding title, but listed in order right after miracle and healing ministries in the above text. The Greek word translated "helps" means "to lay hold of, so as to support." In other words, a minister of helps is someone who commits himself to another ministry in order to support and assist in any way he or she can.

I'm impressed by the ministry team of Billy Graham in this respect. One of the great reasons for his enormous success has to be the dedicated team that has worked with him since the early '50s—Cliff Barrows, George Beverly Shea, and others, have been with him from the very beginning. *They didn't see their work with Billy as a stepping stone towards their own independent ministries, but rather as a lifetime calling. And in the process of helping his ministry, they have achieved personal ministerial success that they never could have attained on their own. How many records has Bev Shea sold, how many millions of people has Barrows taught over the years, that never would have been possible outside of Billy Graham's ministry? When you commit yourself to the ministry of helps you lay hold of personal success that you might never have achieved otherwise.*" (Emphasis mine)

Is there a Barnabas, a Silas, a Timothy, an Aquila/Priscilla reading that is ready to serve the next Apostle Paul?

Or a band of mighty men ready to serve the next David?

An Elisha to serve the next Elijah?

Or the next Kenneth Copeland that will serve the book table of the next Oral Roberts?

God has ordained an amazing journey for you and secret number one to experiencing this incredible blessing is settling the question once and for all – yes, as a New Testament Christian, I am called to serve another man's ministry.

SECRET
2

The Secret of Honor

I knew a man very well that went to work for a major ministry. He quickly worked his way into a position of leadership in the ministry. Whenever he was in the presence of the president of the ministry he was the picture of honor. From serving the man water, juice, etc... to buckling him in his car, to displaying the most incredible outward show of honor and respect once could imagine. But when he was not in the presence of the mentor he would second guess and make ever increasing disparaging remarks.

This man had a hidden agenda. He was operating under the deception that he would one day take this man's ministry, which sadly he eventually attempted to do through a five year series of frivolous and totally unsuccessful lawsuits against his mentor.

Today this man is completely out of the ministry while the mentor is thriving, reaching the world for Christ. Honor is much more than an outward display or lip service.

We serve a God who puts a high premium on the character trait of honor. Yet we live in a day where there is an apparent dearth of honor both inside and outside the church. Simply defined honor is high respect toward someone or something.

It has been my honor to serve as the Vice-President of Ministries for Dr. Morris Cerullo for nearly three decades.

How can we expect the blessing of God as we serve another person's ministry without a heart felt, abiding, sincere honor and respect for our mentor?

Honor is referred to directly or indirectly over 400 times in scripture as a command in both our horizontal (with our spouse, employer, children, those in authority, etc) and in our vertical (with God the Father, the Son and the Holy Spirit) relationships.

Every dysfunction can be traced to a lack of honor for authority.

The first commandment with promise is "Honor thy mother and father that your days may be long upon the land your God is giving you"

Exodus 20:12

A great man once said, "All truth is parallel".

Not only will we be blessed in the "land" that God has given us when we honor our natural parents, but the same honor is a condition of God's blessing as it relates to our spiritual leaders. We live in a generation that openly celebrates dishonor and disrespect.

II Timothy 3:1-2 foretold our day:

"This know also, that in the last days perilous times shall come. For men shall be lovers of their own selves, covetous, boasters, proud; blasphemers, disobedient to parents, unthankful, unholy, without natural affection, trucebreakers, false accusers, incontinent..."

Sad to say that dishonor and second guessing of our leaders runs rampant in the church today. Something as simple as referring to our pastor by his or her title and not simply on a "buddy buddy" first name basis that so many today feel is appropriate under the misguided belief that there is no difference between the laity and the clergy.

Do you think over familiarity with your spiritual leader/mentor can lead to disrespect? It did for Aaron and Miriam. (Num 12:1-2) And the Lord called Aaron and Miriam to task on it immediately!

"They (Aaron and Miriam) said, 'Has the Lord spoken only through Moses? Hasn't He spoken through us too?' But the Lord heard them... So immediately the Lord called out to Moses, Aaron and Miriam and said, "Go out to the tabernacle, all three of you! And the Lord said to them, 'Now listen to what I have to say!"

The Bible tells us that the Lord was very angry with them, and struck Miriam with leprosy!

Some of the most "super spiritual" believers are the ones that have the biggest struggle with honoring their leaders as they feel that they have arrived and are on equal footing with anyone. While it is true that we are equal in relationship to God, we are different in function, and God expects that difference to be honored.

God expected it of the children of Israel and He still expects it today.

A return to biblical honor of our spiritual leaders is an indispensable key that will begin to release a new dimension of the blessing of God into your life, your family and your ministry.

SECRET
3

The Secret of Obedience

After the secret of honor is in place, which we said is a sincere respect that comes from the heart, the character trait of obedience will naturally follow.

Obedience is coming under the authority of your mentor. In other words, submission.

Elisha came under the authority of Elijah and received the blessing of the double portion:

> *"And so it was, when they had crossed over, that Elijah said to Elisha, Ask! What may I do for you, before I am taken away from you? Elisha said, Please let a double portion of your spirit be upon me. So he said, you have asked a hard thing. Nevertheless, if you see me when I am taken from you, it shall be so for you; but if not, it shall not be so"*
>
> 2 Kings 2:9-10

Elijah's charge to Elisha, "If you see me when I am taken from you..." speaks of Elisha staying connected to his mentor and paying close attention to his mentor.

Let me share a true story that illustrates the blessing of obedience to your mentor...

For years God had been speaking to Brother Cerullo's heart that a time was coming that He was going to use our ministry to shake the nation of Spain.

Sure enough the time came and I received an invitation from a precious pastor in Madrid asking if Brother Cerullo would come to the Spanish capital.

I immediately got on a plane and met with this wonderful group of about 12 pastors from across Madrid. One pastored a church of 20 people, another 35, the largest was less than 200...

All together these twelve pastors had a combined attendance of maybe 600 people.

They were inviting Brother Cerullo to come and conduct a crusade in a beautiful auditorium in the center of Madrid that seated 1,200. Their faith was so high and they were so excited. This would be the biggest charismatic meeting any of them had ever heard of in Spain up to that time. The purity and sincerity of these men so touched my heart...

As per our policy, I always call Brother Cerullo before leaving a city to give him a report.

As I shared the exciting report, Dr Cerullo said "Greg, God showed me this crusade would be in a bull ring. Go back to the pastors and share with them what God is speaking to my heart."

I went back to these men with these words and you could see their hearts and their heads sink in fear at the challenge of filling a bull ring.

They asked if Brother Cerullo would come and conduct the meeting in the auditorium first and then build toward a larger meeting in a bull ring the following year.

I knew what the prophet of God had communicated and with all the kindness and sensitivity I could muster I assured the pastors that as God had spoken to Brother Cerullo, it would come to pass...

I had seen it too many times before...

I extended my stay in Madrid and reluctantly they took me to look at bull rings in Madrid. We settled on a brand new bull ring with a retractable roof called "La Cubierta", which translated means "the covering". La Cubierta seated 12,000 people!

Well the day of the crusade came.

The pastors met me early for prayer and to help organize the set up.

Then we had our ushers and workers meeting at 4PM.

At 5PM we opened the doors as the pastors were now seated on the platform praying and hoping for the best!

To their shock and amazement the people began to stream in two hours before the meeting was scheduled to begin.

And the stream didn't stop...

By 6PM there was not a vacant seat in the La Cubierta bull ring!

CNN was there...

These pastors' eyes were as wide as saucers and their spirits were soaring as high as an eagle. Little did we all know we hadn't seen anything yet...

As the powerful anointing of the Holy Spirit and the sound of Spanish praise and worship filled the covered bull ring, I introduced Brother Cerullo.

"I greet you tonight in the Name that is above every name, Jesus Christ the Son of the Living God", Brother Cerullo proclaimed as he held his Bible high for all to see.

A few moments later as Brother Cerullo continued to preach under a mighty anointing he declared "Spain does not belong to the devil, but Spain belongs to Jesus!"

As those words left his lips a phenomenon I will never forget took place...

Golf ball sized hail began to pelt the platform and the entire audience that were assembled inside this *covered* bull ring!!

I looked up to the heavens and all I could see were sheets of white hail continuing to fall for several uninterrupted minutes. Yes, hail stones were falling inside a *covered* bull ring!

Brother Cerullo did not miss a beat. He continued to minister as though the conditions were perfect.

I covered Mrs. Cerullo head with my jacket. Soon plastic was over the sound equipment and keyboard. Umbrellas popped up all over the bull ring. The prophet of God continued to preach.

Finally the hail subsided. I was now able to see that the roof was most certainly in place the whole time. There was no other explanation: the hail was nothing less than a supernatural sign and manifestation from Jehovah!

Finally acknowledging this unusual occurrence, Morris prophesied, "The hail that fell in this arena is a sign of the blessing of God on the nation of Spain!"

The crowd erupted in spontaneous praise. Over 10,000 souls came to Christ that night. Hundreds of wonderful physical healings swept the audience. Those pastors, the church, and Spain would never be the same again...

2001 Morris Cerullo Madrid, Spain Crusade

And it all started with one of the most important secrets that will unlock the blessing of God over your life and ministry...obedience!

SECRET
4

The Secret of Flexibility

Blessed are the flexible!

There may not be a greater secret to success in serving another persons ministry than being willing to be flexible.

In the first chapter I told the exciting story of how I encountered God on the bridge – how He called me in that chapel service to stand by Dr Cerullo's side and to help him in the ministry, etc...

Then when I left the ORU chapel that Spring morning, I was certain after my experience with God that when I called the Morris Cerullo World Evangelism offices I would immediately be asked to travel and minister with Dr Cerullo.

Not exactly how it worked out!

"All the ministry positions are filled, but we did just post a job opening for a cost accountant", I was advised by the MCWE Personnel Manager, Glandon Broome.

Now I had transferred into ORU after two years studying at the University of Notre Dame, where I was on a full academic scholarship. When I met with the ORU Admissions Office I asked them to evaluate my credits and advise me the best track to pursue that would utilize my Notre Dame credits to the fullest.

I was advised to transfer into a major in Business Administration. I chose Accounting. But from day one I said to myself (and to the Lord), I will study Accounting but I will never be an accountant!

I was at ORU to be prepared to reach the world for Jesus, not to be an accountant!

Now with Glandon on the other end of the phone line telling me about the accounting position, I felt I could relate to Job: the thing I had greatly feared was coming upon me!

I reluctantly let him know that I was about to graduate in a few weeks time with a degree in accounting and that he could send me an application.

I was hired less than a week later.

My first two years at MCWE I served as a cost accountant. I grew to love it. God helped me discover a State of California tax law that retroactively returned to the ministry tens of thousands of dollars in taxes paid on printing that MCWE was exempt from.

On the weekends I carried a ten foot cross around the city of San Diego. Soon one of the newspapers carried a story which Dr Cerullo happened to see. One day in the interoffice mail I received a personal handwritten note from Dr Cerullo letting me know how proud he and Theresa were of me. Soon I was invited to speak in our weekly MCWE chapel.

A few weeks later I was called into the office of the VP of Accounting. He informed me that Dr Cerullo wanted me to pray about a move. I thought it was an organizational move, but to my surprise it was an offer to move me and our family to London to head up our European office and ministry outreaches.

I served as the European Director for MCWE for six years. During these years, the communist curtain came down and Dr Cerullo was the first to be invited to Moscow to conduct a three day crusade from the Olympic Stadium that saw over 50,000 attend and gave their lives to Christ in three nights. The nation was shaken.

While I served in Europe, MCWE was the first Christian organization to be granted a license to broadcast in the UK and Europe. As a result millions were reached by our Victory program on the European Super Channel.

God spoke to Brother Cerullo about launching Mission To London, which for six consecutive years drew capacity crowds for our one-week long events at the world famous 16,000 seat Earl's Court Auditorium and shook Great Britain to the core. Many of Britain's mega churches of today were born in Mission to London.

The Eastern European nations opened to Dr Cerullo. It was during a preliminary visit I was making to Bucharest, Romania to meet with pastors that through a series of miracles I was spontaneously given the opportunity to preach to 200,000 demonstrators that were convened in the University Plaza in the heart of the Romanian capital.

I was the first believer to ever address this demonstration with a gospel message, which was a nightly occurrence in the wake of Caucescu's overthrow and execution. I was told that for months after I left, every night a time was given for the demonstrators to hear a gospel message from a local pastor.

The breakthroughs I have been privileged to be a part of would not have been possible if I hadn't been willing to be flexible and say yes to the opportunity to serve as an accountant and enable God to plant me in the place that He would cause me to prosper and fulfill His purposes.

And flexibility will always continue to be a secret of releasing the blessing and favor of God as you serve another persons ministry. Being called upon to do things that will only succeed with God's help and blessing will stretch you and grow you if you don't avoid those opportunities to serve when they are presented.

Like when Dr Cerullo asked me on a one day notice to be his on air co-host for our worldwide prayer reality program "Helpline" that for three years was filmed from CBS Studios and received over 1.5 million calls for prayer, with tens of thousands praying the prayer of salvation for the first time.

On the set of Morris Cerullo Helpline

Those that know me know that I have never sought after or been comfortable to be in the forefront. To be asked to carry the co host duties for Helpline, emcee our major events, lead singing, etc – all have been challenges to me to move out of my comfort zone, be obedient, be flexible – and then watch the blessing of God flow again and again.

Secret #4: Be flexible. Then watch the miracles of God flow as you follow Him into unchartered new territory. Blessed are the flexible. Step by step, each step will be a miracle!

SECRET
5

The Secret of Faithfulness

While we live in a world that celebrates jumping from one relationship to the next, faithfulness has taken a back seat to self interest. And sad to say the church world appears to be not far behind as Christians hop from one church, from one ministry, and one message to the next. All motivated by the bottom line — what's in it for me and what's best for me.

Like honor, faithfulness is big in God's eyes yet certainly not valued highly in the day and age we live in.

Faithfulness is defined as "adhering firmly and devotedly, as to a person, cause or idea; steady in allegiance or affection; loyal; constant".

Proverbs 20:6 asks it this way:

> *"Most men will proclaim every one his own goodness:* ***but a faithful man who can find?"***

I Corinthians 4:2 says:

> *"Also it is required first in a minister that a man be found faithful"*

Proverbs 28:20 promises...

> *"A faithful man shall abound with blessings..."*

And Matthew 25:12 (NKJV)...

His lord said to him, 'Well done, good and faithful servant; you were faithful over a few things, I will make you ruler over many things. Enter into the joy of your lord.'

By the grace of God, 2013 commemorates my 26th anniversary of answering the call to stand by the side of Dr. Morris Cerullo.

Have there been times that my commitment to the relationship has been tested over a quarter of a century? To say that there haven't been would be unrealistic.

The key to faithfulness is knowing the will and the calling of God.

Someone once said, you are either called or you are crazy!

If God called you to serve another man's ministry, if God called you to marry your spouse, you can always go back to that original calling as the bedrock of your commitment to faithfulness, especially during the trying times. Above all your commitment to faithfulness is not only to another person but it is first and foremost to the high calling of God in Christ Jesus for your life.

One of the great statements Jesus ever made calls us to be faithful in serving another persons ministry:

"And if you have not been faithful in that which is another man's, who shall give you that which is your own?"

Luke 16:21

While this verse clearly lays down the divine qualification for receiving that which is your own, I personally have never viewed this scripture as a license to see my service to Dr Cerullo as some kind of spring board to my own ministry.

Over the years I have turned down many opportunities that I felt could be seen as taking advantage of the platform that Dr Cerullo has entrusted to me.

I have simply preferred under God to endeavor to remain single minded and to stay faithful one day at a time to His call and to His servant, and have already received so much more in the process than I could ever have asked or hoped for.

I know, and you can too, that your future will take care of itself as you remain faithful to God, His kingdom and to your mentor.

> *"But seek ye first the kingdom of God and His righteousness and all these things shall be added unto you"*
>
> Matt 6:33

God is looking for a few faithful men and women...and I believe you are one! What a reward it will be when you hear these eternal words on that Great Day, *"Well done good and faithful servant...enter into the joy of thy Lord"* (Matt 25:21).

SECRET
6

The Secret of Being Proactive

One of the great privileges and most rewarding opportunities you can experience serving another man's ministry is found in the secret of being a proactive servant.

A proactive person is defined as one who "creates or controls a situation by causing something to happen rather than responding to it after it has happened".

A fruitful, effective disciple is much more than an order taker. After proving yourself faithful over time a foundation of trust is established which is the key ingredient required to move from a relationship of simple service to becoming a proactive partner.

I will never forget Moscow, 1989.

For 14 consecutive years prior, from the platform of the world renowned Royal Albert Hall, Dr Cerullo prophesied Russia's iron curtain would come down and the Soviet Union would open in an unprecedented way to the preaching of the gospel.

In the late 1980's that is precisely what began to happen as a movement for the democratization of the Soviet Union referred to as "Perestroika" was being championed by then General Secretary of the Communist Party, Mikhail Gorbachev.

The beep of the fax machine at my desk in our European office in the Fall of 1989, signaled an incoming communication. As I began to read, I discovered that it was an invitation from the President of the Russian Pentecostal Union, Rev Bilas Roman, asking Brother Cerullo to be the first to come to Moscow in the Perestroika era to conduct an open public crusade.

Immediately I shared the invitation with Brother Cerullo and made flight arrangements to meet with Rev Bilas and his leaders to begin to make the plans for this historic invitation.

We settled on a date in December at the historic 7,000 seat Izmailovo Auditorium in the outskirts of Moscow.

When the time came, I arrived in Moscow with Dr Cerullo the day before as he was scheduled to appear on the Moscow News that evening. An interview that was set to fill a one or two minute segment was mightily visited by the presence of God and extended to nearly 30 minutes! The host was so deeply touched that she asked Dr Cerullo to pray for the viewers to receive the miracle of salvation, and then followed that with a request for Dr Cerullo to pray for all viewers that were in need of physical healing.

The phones there at the news station immediately were jammed with callers testifying to God's saving and healing power. God was beginning to shake the nation right before our eyes...

That night when our interpreter returned to his apartment, he was met by his elderly atheist neighbor who waited for him to return, to testify that when Dr Cerullo prayed, she experienced a deep heat in her back and an immediate healing from years of a debilitating spinal condition! Right there on her porch, she prayed with our translator to receive Christ as Savior!

The next afternoon even after opening the doors three hours early and filling the Izmailovo to capacity, the crowds were still ten-deep encircling the entire arena with great expectancy and frustration that they could not get in.

The police insisted that the church leaders convince Dr Cerullo to cancel the meeting so that they could disperse the people, who had now begun to damage the property, breaking panes of glass, etc, in an effort to force themselves into the building.

The top leaders approached me and requested to speak with Dr Cerullo about the security problems and to make the request that he postpone the meeting.

My job was to not disturb Dr Cerullo with a negative report before a meeting, but to simply solve it myself so that he is able to stay focused and uninterrupted prior to the service.

This was an opportunity for me to be proactive and not disturb the servant of God who was in his customary time of prayer, fasting and preparation for the meeting.

With the Russian leaders standing before me shaken, I quietly prayed for God's wisdom.

Here's what I recommended to the leaders:

What if we take the many boxes containing 5,000 brand new Bibles we had delivered in the arena to give to the new converts, and take them outside to the people that couldn't get in with the promise that Dr Cerullo would come back to Moscow again soon in a larger stadium for another meeting?

The leaders shook their heads in agreement. We handed the boxes of Bibles to the police who brought them out to the people. The people scooped the Bibles up as if they had just won the lottery! They were happy to receive them and peace was restored when they heard that Dr Cerullo would return to Moscow for another meeting in the near future.

That night was one of the most glorious services I have ever been a part of. As Brother Cerullo brought the simple message of the gospel, nearly all of the 7,000 present received the greatest miracle in all the world, the miracle of forgiveness of sins and the healing of their souls through the salvation of the blood of Jesus Christ!

Several months later we returned to Moscow, this time in the 15,000 seat Olympic Stadium, for three capacity nights – nearly 50,000 precious Russians combined giving their lives to Christ!

Morris Cerullo 1990 Moscow Crusade at Olympic Stadium

The Apostle Paul said, *"I have planted, Apollos watered, but God gave the increase. So then neither is he that planteth anything, neither he that watereth, but God that giveth the increase"* (I Cor 3:6-7)

As the mentor/mentee relationship grows over time, you will know the heart of the man or woman you are serving and what he or she would expect in certain situations.

This knowledge makes you a much more valuable servant and you are able to move from a place of simply waiting for instructions to becoming a creative contributor to the overall vision and purpose of your leader and their ministry.

While Dr Cerullo is the unquestioned visionary and strong spiritual leader of MCWE, one of his great strengths as a mentor is his humility and expectation that his key team members operate with an authority and spiritual license to bring their creative ideas and input to the table on any and all aspects of the ministry.

It takes the investment and trust of a great mentor to know when and how much authority his servant can successfully be released to handle.

A man can only truly be responsible and accountable for the success of that which he perceives he has authority for.

Some of the most successful outreaches of MCWE were a result of the synergy between Dr Cerullo and our team that fueled our passion and creativity to bring "God ideas" and suggestions to our leader.

However a word to the wise: Don't think about bringing an idea that you are not willing to become responsible to personally carry out!

Are you ready to take your next step in serving another person's ministry? If there is a need in your church or ministry that you see is not being filled, maybe it is God calling you to be proactive and volunteer to fill it — and not waiting for someone else to do so — or for you to be asked!

Now is your season to soar as a proactive servant!

In the next chapter we will talk about the privilege and importance of receiving the impartation of your mentor, which will never happen until you move into a relationship where you can be released to stretch your giftings and be a proactive servant as an extension of your mentor.

SECRET
7

Receiving The Mantle of Your Mentor

"And Elijah took his mantle, and wrapped it together, and smote the waters, and they were divided hither and thither, so that the two went over on dry ground. And it came to pass, when they were gone over, that Elijah said to Elisha, Ask what I shall do for thee, before I be taken away from thee. And Elisha said, I pray thee, let a double portion of thy spirit be upon me. And he said, Thou hast asked a hard thing; nevertheless, if thou see me when I am taken from thee, it shall be so unto thee; but if not, it shall not be so."

2 Kings 2:8-10

After endeavoring to show yourself faithful in serving your mentor by incorporating the secrets I outline in the preceding six chapters, the mentee then qualifies him or herself to experience the greatest blessing of serving another man's ministry: the awesome privilege and opportunity of receiving a portion of their mentor's mantle into your own life and ministry.

In the blessed experience and process of receiving your mentor's mantle, it's not just for your personal benefit and blessing. Receiving the mantle and blessing of your mentor makes you a more effective servant and extension of their ministry. In fact, you really can't effectively serve and represent your mentor without an impartation of the giftings and anointing that God has placed in your mentor upon your life and ministry.

A great mentor is not primarily motivated by what they can get out of their mentee but ultimately what they can impart.

This is where I think so much depends on the heart and vision of your mentor and why this book is not just written to the one who serves another man's ministry but also to ministry leaders that are served and supported by those that have been entrusted to their mentorship.

I have been incredibly blessed to have had the opportunity for the past twenty five years to serve a man with a giving, father's heart of impartation. Dr Cerullo's heartbeat and life mission is to pass on the anointing from his life. Through the years, I have recognized, appreciated, valued and coveted this impartation from Dr Cerullo's life.

And as great as the impartation of the anointing for ministry has been, there has been so much more. The impartation of wisdom and compassion in dealing with people, places and things in everyday life has been invaluable. Something as mundane as making a reservation at a restaurant can become a teaching moment!

I have an important question for the reader that is serving another man's ministry. What are you willing to put into the relationship and what do you really want to get out of the relationship?

In his relationship with Elijah, Elisha valued above all else the anointing and mantle upon Elijah's life.

It wasn't the limelight, a promotion or a bigger pay check that Elisha asked for, it was for a double portion of the anointing that was upon Elijah's life!

I encourge you to draw from the example and the anointing that is upon your mentor.

While there has been a price to pay, I have known all along that while giving my best to live by the seven secrets outlined in this book, that ultimately Dr Cerullo and Theresa have always been more committed to me getting more out of our relationship than I would ever put in, which I have...

This is why I believe that an adventure – a blessing unlike any blessing – awaits the man or woman that will answer the call and then follow these seven secrets of serving another mans ministry.

Allow me to pray with you:

"Father, I lift my friend to you today. I ask you to reward them as they diligently seek to serve you and your kingdom. Release a fresh anointing of your power and love into their life and ministry today in Jesus name, Amen!"

Postscript: Legacy

During the past year since I began writing this book, there have been some very profound and very exciting developments that have materialized directly related to the future of Dr. Cerullo's ministry and the message of this book...

Just a few months ago, a dream that Morris has secretly carried for more than 25 years is becoming a reality right before our eyes... The establishment of a Morris Cerullo World Outreach Legacy Training Center on 18 prime acres in the beautiful Mission Valley corridor of San Diego will ensure that this very ministry that has been singularly used to raise up millions of national Christian leaders worldwide, will continue and will never die!

Artists rendition of World Outreach Legacy Training Center

The Morris Cerullo International Center, Mission Valley Campus will be the focal point for carrying out an incredible 20/2020 vision – to equip and train 20 million nationals by the year 2020! This incredible campus will carry out the mandate "Son Build Me An Army" until Jesus comes!

For more information and how you can be a part visit: www.mcwe.com/legacy

What Key Christian Leaders Are Saying About "The Blessing of Serving Another Man's Ministry"

Greg Mauro has spent the majority of his life defining what it means to have integrity, faithfulness, and commitment. This book will show the importance of a servant's heart, and how even though one's work may go unseen, their role is important and their impact is great. For anyone who needs a reminder of the joys and rewards of living a faithful life, I would highly recommend this work.

— Pastor Matthew Barnett,
Co-founder of the Dream Center

"For many years I have been amazed at the level of competence with which Greg Mauro has served Dr. Morris Cerullo. Every minister of the gospel should be so blessed as Dr. Cerullo has been through the gifted service of this man of God. In this book the blessings of servant leadership are made so abundantly clear. As you read, drink deeply of the spirit of Greg Mauro. Your life will be the richer and your blessings the greater as you are exposed to a contemporary example of servant living. Enjoy!"

— J. Don George, *Sr. Pastor*
Calvary Church Irving, Texas

Greg Mauro has had the privilege of walking side by side with a true General. As Elisha spent 10 years serving and learning from Elijah, Greg has spent over 20 years serving Dr Morris Cerullo. He teaches that serving another mans dream is not only fulfilling but can lead to your own dreams being fulfilled. Good going Greg, you made me want to serve even more!

— Dr. Tim Storey

It is my honor and privilege to recommend "The Blessing of Serving Another Man's Ministry" by Greg Mauro. I am convinced that the Christian Church has inadvertently taught that unless someone is the main or set man, they are of no value. For 25 years, Greg has walked behind Dr. Cerullo, sharing the burden of international ministry and has freed him to follow God's voice and vision.

— Dr. Stephen L. Lowery, *President*
National Church of God and National
Bible College & SeminaryWashington, DC

"The Blessing Of Serving Another Mans Ministry" is a mini book with a mega punch. This a must read, for every believer that feels or knows that they have being called to serve in any way. Thanks Rev. Greg for letting others glean from your experience and wisdom.

— Apostle (Dr.) Mike Efe Zino

As the hispanic voice for Dr. Morris Cerullo for many years, I have not ever known a man, anointed and called by God, that has served with such passion, intensification, and loyalty, another anointed man's ministry like Greg Mauro has stood side by side with God's Apostle Morris Cerullo. Greg has written in this book such powerful secrets of deep revelation regarding the calling to serve others, that any one that reads this book will never again refuse to serve another man's ministry.

— Dr. Hernan Castano

Greg Mauro has been the right-hand man to Evangelist Morris Cerullo for many years. Each time I have met with him I have been impressed by his very efficient servant-hood and his sincere desire to make life easier for Brother Cerullo. The secrets to tapping into the blessing he has written about in this book are tried and tested through his years of serving. God bless you, Greg, for writing such a book!

— Stephan K. Munsey, *Ph.D. Sr. Pastor,*
Family Christian Center, Munster, Indiana